# Amazing Grace

## Joi Jackson

Copyright © 2014 by Joi Jackson

*Amazing Grace*
by Joi Jackson

Printed in the United States of America

ISBN 9781498407175

All rights reserved solely by the author. The author guarantees all contents are original and do not infringe upon the legal rights of any other person or work. No part of this book may be reproduced in any form without the permission of the author. The views expressed in this book are not necessarily those of the publisher.

Scripture quotations are taken from the New International Version (NIV). Copyright © 1985 by Edwin H. Palmer. Also used the New Living Translation (NLT). Copyright © 1996 by Tyndale House Publishers.

www.xulonpress.com

Dedicated to My Heavenly Father,

My First Love

And All of My Little Replicas

# Foreword

As Esther sits relaxing on the beach, she thinks over her life and how she got to this point. The full moon is bright and shining and the tide is high. The waves are splashing against the rocks and the beams of the pier. She contemplates jumping in to finally be free from the strife that has consumed her for all of her life. She has been sitting here for what seems like days but in fact it's only been 3 hours. She has watched the families picnicking. A little girl no more than 3 years old runs to the shoreline and is chased back towards her dad by the ocean waves. A little boy chases baby seagulls along the beach and when he gets too far from his mother, she calls him back and he comes running into her arms. The family packs up and leaves and the sun set with vibrant colors of purple, pink, and orange. She knows that God is real every time she thinks of the splendor and wonder that is God. She can't help but wonder if God is real, then why had she suffered so much pain and anguish in her lifetime. Nightfall comes and she sees her reflection in the water. She marvels at how the years and pain have added wrinkles to her face and hands. Her hair once black and flowing is now gray and leaving. Her womb once alive and in full season is now closed and she is barren. Finally the contemplation becomes more than a thought and is now her jumping off the pier into the raging ocean. As her feet leave the wood of the pier, her mind begins to reflect on her life....

# Chapter One

## *Happy Birthday*

"Okay, Naomi on your next pain bear down and push with all of your might", says the midwife. Naomi pushes with all of her strength and the color drains from her face as she experiences the worse pain known to mankind. Suddenly Naomi notices the midwife's face and that she looks afraid. "Naomi, don't push anymore no matter what labor pains you feel. Listen to me carefully because this is very important to you and your baby. I am going to place my hand inside of you to try and turn your baby because she is coming out bottom first", said the midwife. Naomi screamed in agony as the pains of labor racked her body and the midwife's hand seemed to tear her soul from her body. Naomi could only think that this baby would be the death of her as she struggled to remain conscious through the pain. She began to remember the joy she felt when she brought her first born Samuel home. Her husband Isaiah was so overcome with joy that he began to cry. Thinking on the happy times helped Naomi get through the pain that consumed her.

She was snapped back to reality by the voice of the midwife yelling, "Push Naomi, Now!" Naomi pushed with everything she had left in her. Relief instantly overcame her as she felt the baby leave her body but was immediately replaced with fear as she didn't hear the baby crying. Naomi was exhausted and very weak but she didn't care. Her only concern was for her baby as she leaned forward to see what was going on. The midwife was taking the cord from around the baby that appeared to be purple in color. Panic set in as Naomi wondered if her baby was alive or not and as the midwife unwrapped and severed the cord, panic was replaced with joy and gratitude as her baby began to move and cry. The midwife wrapped the baby and sent for Isaiah to meet his beautiful new baby girl. Isaiah walked through the curtain to see his exhausted wife Naomi holding a beautifully swaddled baby in her arms and as he bent to embrace them both he whispered to his wife, "Esther, because she has travailed and she will save us."

# Chapter Two

# *It's the Little Things*

The sun was warm on her face as Esther rode on the shoulders of her father. The wind blew just enough so that the sun wouldn't burn her. It was like God was gently breathing on her and showering her with His love. "Daddy, daddy swing me around again", five year old Esther said as she and her father chased her older brother Samuel around the yard. Samuel laughed and ran as hard as he could. He was determined not to allow his dad and sister to catch him. He zigged when they zagged and ran circles all around them. Isaiah lowered Esther to the ground despite her protests and she began to make mud pies. She used dirt and spit to make the pie and pulled grass and yellow flowers from the ground to place on top of the mud pies to make them look good. Just as Isaiah placed Esther on the ground, the screen door slammed closed and the voice of Naomi could be heard along with the giggles of young Ruth as Naomi watched and adored her family playing together.

Isaiah ran towards Naomi and Ruth, wrapped his arms around them both and whispered, "I love my life and wouldn't change it for the world. God has truly blessed me above what I ever asked or thought possible." All of the pain that she had endured to birth her babies into the world was worth it and she couldn't think of any place else that she would rather be either. She loved Isaiah with all of her heart. She reminisced on the days when their love was new before the children were born. She remembered late nights spent talking and learning more about each other. She remembered the way Isaiah fought for her when her father said they were too young to become so serious. All those nights spent planning their lives together and helping each other reach the dreams they had. They vowed never to forget the way they felt in the beginning when their love was new. Each day they made sure to communicate with each other all of the intimacies their lives had brought. Even on the hard days when life threw them a curve ball, they remembered their love for one another and persevered through it together.

As she watched her babies, she remembered the time when they were afraid they would never have the family they wanted because she had miscarried the first time. They spent countless nights crying together, trying to figure out what went wrong, mourning the loss, and eventually coming to grips with the reality that God knows best. That was the hardest pill to swallow because they had never suffered a loss like that before. However, even with the pain and heartache, Naomi and Isaiah never gave up hope because they knew that God would give them a special gift. After the many heartbreak suffered, their faith in God was stronger than ever. The night that Naomi conceived Samuel was after they had travailed in prayer asking God to make them whole and to bless her womb. All of these things flowed through her mind as Isaiah stood in front of her and she fell in love all over again.

Isaiah kissed both Naomi and Ruth and ran back towards the kids to continue what he considered to be his fatherly duties. As Naomi watched, Isaiah began to play with the kids and she soon found herself sprawled out on the grass laughing because the kids had somehow managed to tackle both she and Isaiah. Even baby Ruth was laying on top of them caught in the whirlwind of laughter that seemed to make the world go silent and be at peace. None of them had any idea of the storm that was brewing ahead.

## Chapter Three

## *Making Memories*

*A*fter having time to play together as a family each day, Isaiah called everyone together so that they could wash up for supper. Since their marriage, 13 years earlier, Naomi and Isaiah started the tradition of having time to study and learn about God every night before bed. As they began to have children, they continued with the tradition and as the kids became older they allowed them to pick their favorite bible events to be read about on some nights. Isaiah believed this time was important because it gave all of them the opportunity to see how God worked miracles then and to empower them to be courageous enough to believe and ask him to work miracles now. Isaiah learned as a boy that there is nothing that is impossible with God and he wanted to make sure to instill the same teachings in his children.

As Samuel got older, Daniel 3 became his favorite bible event to read about. He loved the fact that the three Hebrew boys were bold enough to say they not bow to any god outside of the one true God and it didn't matter what threats were made against them. Every time he thought about the way God allowed them to be thrown in the fiery furnace and yet not become consumed by it, he knew that all he had to do was pray and God would deliver him from any situation he faced. It taught him courage and that it was okay to be different than others; especially if you are one of God's chosen.

Naomi enjoyed reading the story of Hannah to Samuel because he truly was the child that she prayed for. She made sure from birth that he knew just how special he was and made sure he knew that God had a special plan for him. She had done just as Hannah did when she promised God that if He gave her a son she would give him back to God. After suffering the pain of losing a child, Samuel was all that she could've asked for and yet so much more. Being able to hear the sounds of laughter and cooing brought so much joy to Naomi and Isaiah's lives. They truly learned the love that The Father has for his children. There is no one that can make Him stop loving you and he wants to see you smiling and happy too.

Naomi and Isaiah cherished each moment with Samuel even up until Esther's entrance into their lives.

Esther's favorite bible event was about herself, of course. Since she could talk, she remembered her parents telling her the story of how she was born and why her father named her Esther. In the bible, Esther was raised by her Uncle Mordecai after her parents died. Esther ended up being the queen after her uncle informed her of a plot that was being made to assassinate King Xerxes and she warned him. Haman plotted to have all the Jews in the area killed after her Uncle Mordecai didn't bow to Haman, a prince that King Xerxes gave special honors to. Esther, her maids, and her people fasted for three days before she went before the king without being summoned, risking death, to ask for her people to be spared. The king ended up hanging Haman, appointing Mordecai as his prime minister, and giving the Jews the right to defend themselves against any enemy.

To Esther this meant that she could go before God, her Lord and King, and ask anything and He will favor her and grant her heart's desire. Esther loved the bravery and courage that Esther showed in the bible and being true to her name she had a boldness that only someone with the name Esther could have. Little Ruth had yet to find her favorite biblical event but she giggled and smiled as she listened to her family replay the events that had occurred for so many years before. These nights would serve as the foundation for building a family that God could and would always be honored with. No matter where life took them, they knew the power of what God could do.

# Chapter Four

## *Something's Wrong*

Naomi awoke in the middle of the night to the sound of Isaiah coughing and gagging. She lit the lamp next to the bed and turned over to ask him if he needed any water. She was startled to find there was blood on the sheets. Isaiah never was one that would get sick and so he felt there was no need to go to the doctor. Having worked in the coal mine for 20 years, it never once crossed his mind that something may go wrong. He had seen others leave the mine but he just assumed they either found other work or they had some family illness that took them away from the mine.

So the next day, Isaiah went into town to visit the doctor and find out what was going on. The doctor diagnosed him with lung cancer due to the inhalation of minerals at the mine. Pain entered into Isaiah's heart as he knew there was no cure. He began to question why God would allow something to happen that would take him away from his family that he so dearly loved. He wondered how they would survive once he was gone. Naomi never had to work and what would she do for money? When they took their wedding vows he promised to love, honor, cherish, protect, and provide for her and he got his chance to prove it each time heartache occurred. He had been there for her through the death of her mother, father, and their first born child. He consoled her with his love and shielded her the best he could from all further pain. He prayed without ceasing for God to heal the wounds that these losses brought for her. In time, God did just what he asked him to do. How could he possibly continue to be there, protecting, and providing for his family if he wasn't here anymore?

Isaiah stayed in town for a while after the doctor's visit and walked around trying to gain perspective and control over his emotions. He knew that this wasn't something that he should keep from his wife but he wanted to focus on spending the time he had left enjoying his family not crying over what was to come. As he walked around town contemplating how he would break the news to his wife, the tears began to flow uncontrollably. He couldn't remember a time that he cried that way except for the day he married his beloved Naomi. He cried so hard at how beautiful she was walking down the aisle with wildflowers in her long flowing hair. The Indian that was dominant in her grandmother flowed strongly through her veins. They had grown up together and were best friends for all of their lives. They had no idea when they were younger that they would be walking down the aisle towards each other with tears in their eyes. It was amazing. Even their wedding night was full of joy as they shared an intimacy neither of them had experienced before. That night he promised to always love her that way. And since that day 15 years ago he had kept that promise. Now at 35 he couldn't see himself breaking that promise.

After two hours of walking around and watching the birds soar through town with no cares or worries, he asked God to make his family's life the same way. He prayed that God continue to supply all of their needs according to His riches in glory. That he comfort them today and everyday from henceforth. He prayed that his family would remember all of the good times and the moments they shared. More importantly he prayed that God would use their study time and conversations of the years to show them that He has a master plan and that He really does have their best interests at heart. The last thing that he prayed before he turned and headed for home was that God give him the courage to speak the words that he knew would break his family's heart.

## Chapter Five

## *Broken Promises*

While Isaiah was in town, Naomi was at home praying fervently for things to be okay. She had all the kids fed and they were in their room reading books and coloring. Naomi knew all too well what the power of prayer could do. She had seen it in action throughout her entire life. Naomi knew as Isaiah's wife, she was supposed to bear him up in prayer. Naomi had been praying since Isaiah left to go into town. She was crying out to God so much so that her face was red and she had bruise marks around her eyes from popped blood vessels.

While she was still praying, Isaiah entered the house. He walked directly to the room instead of using his normal welcome of "Honey, I'm home." Naomi knew something was wrong before she even saw him. Isaiah entered the room just as Naomi was getting up off of her knees. He could see that she had been in prayer on his behalf and that her body was weakened and tired but he knew that her spirit was energized and empowered. Isaiah took his wife's hands and led her to the bed to sit down.

Isaiah knelt on his knees and began to kiss her hands and cheeks. He wanted to paint a picture in his mind of how she was so that he would always remember it. He knew once he said the words that were weighing on his heart, nothing would be the same. Naomi looked at him with his swollen and red eyes from what she knew to be crying and she could only imagine what she looked like because she had been doing the same. Isaiah began, "My love, you have given me too much happiness to count. You have birthed each one of my children and shared all of your life and dreams with me. You have been my best friend and my strongest supporter.

Remember when we took our wedding vows and I promised to protect, love, cherish, and provide for you?" Naomi could only nod her head as she attempted to brace herself. "Well, I don't know how much longer I will be able to keep that promise. The doctor says I have lung cancer", he said. Naomi hung her head and began to cry. Her heart was breaking but she knew she had to be strong for her family; the true attributes of a virtuous woman. Naomi could only whisper, "How long did he say?" Isaiah's voice cracked as he responded, "I don't know for sure but not long. But, baby, we can pray together and God will hear us. No matter what He decides, He will be there for us all because He promised never to leave or forsake us."

Naomi and Isaiah decided not to tell the kids because it would only break their hearts. Instead they wanted to allow the kids to enjoy all the time that was left with him. Naomi and Isaiah embraced and together went down on their knees in prayer to ask the Lord to heal Isaiah and to comfort them all during this time of pain. Isaiah ended the prayer, "But not our will, but thy will be done."

Isaiah and Naomi did just as they promised each other and they spent as much time as possible raising their children. Ever so often, Naomi would look at Isaiah and see him hugging the kids tight as if he was trying to savor the feeling. Isaiah use to sleep soundly through the night but Naomi noticed that he would leave their bed in the middle of the night and not return for several hours. One night when Isaiah did this, Naomi waited a little bit and then went to find him.

What she found warmed her heart like nothing else ever could. Isaiah had climbed into bed with the kids; the only thing missing from this picturesque moment was Naomi. Naomi began weeping and whispering silent prayers to God that things could continue to go on this way forever while she stood in the doorway. Isaiah felt his love's heart breaking and awoke suddenly to find her standing in the doorway. Isaiah slid his arms from under Ruth and Esther's heads so he could go to his wife.

"My love, why are you crying?" Isaiah asked. Naomi replied, "I came to check on you and I feared the worst. I feared that something had happened and that I wouldn't get to say goodbye. When I walked in here and saw you with our gifts from God, I was relieved and I couldn't hold it together anymore. It's so hard trying to keep everything together for you and the kids and I don't know when it happened but something inside of my broke. I couldn't imagine my life without you in it. I believe with all of my heart that God will raise you up. He promised to make us a symbol and source of blessings and if you don't make it, that would make Him a liar and that's not a possibility. He is able to do exceedingly, abundantly above all that we could ever wish, hope, think, or pray for. I love you with all of my heart, Isaiah, and I am with you from now until forever." Naomi and Isaiah embraced and walked hand in hand back to their room so that they could spend some quality time with the Father pleading their petition.

responded, "I don't know for sure but not long. But, baby, we can pray together and God will hear us. No matter what He decides, He will be there for us all because He promised never to leave or forsake us."

Naomi and Isaiah decided not to tell the kids because it would only break their hearts. Instead they wanted to allow the kids to enjoy all the time that was left with him. Naomi and Isaiah embraced and together went down on their knees in prayer to ask the Lord to heal Isaiah and to comfort them all during this time of pain. Isaiah ended the prayer, "But not our will, but thy will be done."

Isaiah and Naomi did just as they promised each other and they spent as much time as possible raising their children. Ever so often, Naomi would look at Isaiah and see him hugging the kids tight as if he was trying to savor the feeling. Isaiah use to sleep soundly through the night but Naomi noticed that he would leave their bed in the middle of the night and not return for several hours. One night when Isaiah did this, Naomi waited a little bit and then went to find him.

What she found warmed her heart like nothing else ever could. Isaiah had climbed into bed with the kids; the only thing missing from this picturesque moment was Naomi. Naomi began weeping and whispering silent prayers to God that things could continue to go on this way forever while she stood in the doorway. Isaiah felt his love's heart breaking and awoke suddenly to find her standing in the doorway. Isaiah slid his arms from under Ruth and Esther's heads so he could go to his wife.

"My love, why are you crying?" Isaiah asked. Naomi replied, "I came to check on you and I feared the worst. I feared that something had happened and that I wouldn't get to say goodbye. When I walked in here and saw you with our gifts from God, I was relieved and I couldn't hold it together anymore. It's so hard trying to keep everything together for you and the kids and I don't know when it happened but something inside of my broke. I couldn't imagine my life without you in it. I believe with all of my heart that God will raise you up. He promised to make us a symbol and source of blessings and if you don't make it, that would make Him a liar and that's not a possibility. He is able to do exceedingly, abundantly above all that we could ever wish, hope, think, or pray for. I love you with all of my heart, Isaiah, and I am with you from now until forever." Naomi and Isaiah embraced and walked hand in hand back to their room so that they could spend some quality time with the Father pleading their petition.

# Chapter 6

# *Let the Healing Begin*

Since becoming sick, Isaiah and Naomi decided to spend as much time as possible together as a family. Every weekend they would find something new to do together. Their favorite place to go seemed to be the beach. Almost every weekend when they would ask the kids where they wanted to go the beach would be their reply. They would build sand castles, run along the beach chasing the seagulls and Isaiah even taught Samuel how to skip seashells across the ocean water. These were the moments that Naomi lived for and as time passed these moments became even more precious.

Each morning Isaiah awoke feeling purposeful and encouraged that God would heal him so that he could spend more time with his family. He tried his best not to think about the diagnosis or what would happen if God didn't deliver him from this illness; he only wanted to focus on the here and now. He enjoyed every moment that he could with his wife, his children, and his God. There was not a day that went by that he didn't express his gratitude for life, health, and strength. Several months went by before Isaiah realized that the level of discomfort he previously felt was diminishing. Of course, he didn't want to say anything because he didn't want to get his wife's hopes up only to be let down again. So instead he just went about his daily life duties of providing for his family and being a lover and friend to his wife.

Naomi noticed that she was no longer awakened to the horrifying sounds of Isaiah choking on his own blood. She began to secretly thank God for healing her husband and became overwhelmed each time she thought about how God had seen them through once again. Each day became much more precious and every waking moment spent reminded her of God's love for them. Naomi was petrified to say anything to Isaiah in the hopes that this wasn't a fluke. After having so many bad days she just wanted to relish in the great days they had been having.

For the first time in what seemed like forever, she could finally sleep through the night and not be awakened by the fear that death was lurking around the corner for Isaiah. Even the children seemed to notice a difference and instead of spending their time playing outside with their friends, they wanted to be with their family. They spent many days barbequing and going into town playing at the town waterfall. Studying and reading the bible nightly became that much more important to them all. Watching how God blessed, healed, and delivered His people despite their disobedience gave them even more hope. They knew they had done things right. Sure they were flesh and blood but with God's help they became the chosen people of God and thus heirs to their inheritance; a part of that inheritance being healing. As Isaiah and Naomi spent time together, they had the opportunity to fall deeper in love with each other. Each day was another day that God fulfilled His promise to them and they both were eternally grateful.

# Chapter Seven

## *Too Good to be True*

*O*ver the course of two years, Isaiah regained his strength and was able to go back to work so that he could begin providing for his family yet again. Isaiah had been feeling so good; he felt like a teenager again and Naomi loved every moment of it. That's why it came as a surprise when Isaiah began coughing again in the middle of the night. The only problem was that he couldn't stop coughing and choking on blood.

Naomi jumped up immediately and went to fetch him some water but even that didn't help and she felt helpless. Esther, ever so sensitive to her father because of the bond they shared, awoke from her sleep to the sound of her father coughing. She hadn't been awakened by his coughing for quite some time so it startled her when she heard it. Esther immediately ran into her parents' room to see if there was anything she could do. Naomi began to panic because the hot cloth and cold drink that usually made it easier for him to breathe wasn't providing the same relief. Esther didn't know what was going on with her father because her parents had kept their promise from years earlier not to tell any of the children of his diagnosis.

When Naomi found that nothing was working, she tried to usher Esther out of the room. Isaiah was weakened as he struggled to breathe and relax. Naomi finally gave up trying to get Esther to move because she was just as stubborn as Isaiah was about people and things he cared about. Instead of arguing with Esther to get her to leave, she decided it was more important to focus on her husband and making him more comfortable. Isaiah motioned for Naomi to come near him so that he could try and talk to her in between the coughing. He had been changing colors between red, blue, and his regular pecan tan brown while this coughing spell sought to overtake him.

Isaiah was exhausted but as Naomi neared him, he whispered to her in a raspy breath, "I love you with all of my heart. You have made me happier than I could've dreamed possible. I will carry our love with me forever. Please don't cry for me because God has a greater plan for us than we even had for ourselves. He already has given me more time and love than I ever could've deserved. Honey, I'm home." Naomi whispered between sobs, "Baby don't talk like that. You don't have to go. He healed you before; He is more than able to heal you again. I love you, baby, stay with me. But it was too late, the coughing had ceased and Isaiah was gone.

## Chapter Eight
## *A Bond Like No Other*

Naomi leaned over Isaiah's body and kissed him through sobs. Naomi thought of a love that she never thought possible but that God decided she should have anyway. Naomi remembered how Isaiah came into her life like a storm. She had been molested by her uncle for years and thought it was impossible for men not to hurt her. She had grown numb to the feelings that men tried to inflict upon her. Isaiah's love took her suddenly and before she knew it she was caught in his whirlwind. Who knew that the day would come when she would have to learn how to live without it? The love Isaiah gave came directly from God. She knew with every fiber of her being that the love she and Isaiah shared was the closest love she could experience on earth that could compare to what God felt for her. Naomi whispered softly, "How can I say goodbye to a love I never thought would ever come? How can I let go of something I never thought would've existed?" Naomi's heart broke apart that night and she knew she would never love the same way again.

Before Naomi could turn to Esther, she already understood what had just happened. Even though she was only 14 years old, the world went silent and she knew it would never be awakened again. Esther went numb as her mother sobbed in anguish and pain. All that Naomi could think was how this man that she loved with all of her heart could be gone. How could God have forsaken her and taken the very thing from her that meant everything? What would she do to take care of her family and provide for them? How would they go on?

All of the pain and grief flooded over them both at once and both Esther and Naomi held on to each other for dear life as they sobbed at the loss of someone so near and dear to them both. Naomi knew that when morning came she would have to call the doctor and make arrangements for Isaiah but for tonight she couldn't deal with that. She had lost the love of her life and she would never see him again on earth. No longer could she pretend that this day would not come so that she could enjoy the days with her loves, she now was staring the realization in the face and there was no way to escape. Neither Esther nor Naomi knew when but at some point 17 year old Samuel and 11 year old Ruth came into the room and before they knew it the whole family was crowded around Isaiah and sobbing from grief. Naomi sobbed for a love that is lost and the children sobbed for the father they lost.

Isaiah's funeral passed in a blur. Family and town people showed up to offer their condolences and support for Naomi and the kids. She truly was touched to find out that so many people cared for him. It still didn't take the sting out of the loss but it made it a little more bearable.

# Chapter Nine

# *Life Goes On*

Naomi took on a job cleaning houses for elderly ladies. This job helped to put food on the table for Esther, Ruth, and Samuel. It wasn't easy managing the kids, the house, and all the bills but Naomi was trying her best. Most days as long as she stayed busy, she didn't even think about how much she missed Isaiah. However, in those lone moments when all was still and quiet, the loneliness overtook her.

Many nights she lay in the spot her husband normally laid in and cried herself to sleep while silently wishing that she would awaken and all of this would be a dream. She prayed with all of her might that God would bring Isaiah back to her. The harder she prayed the more lonesome she seemed to feel. Naomi screamed at God in the moments when she was alone. "I thought you loved me! You promised to be here for me. Where are you? Why have you forsaken me?" It seemed that the harder Naomi cried, the more evident it became that the God she knew and worshipped had left her alone. She was so consumed by her own despair that she didn't notice Esther and Samuel standing at her door hugging each other and sobbing quietly.

Esther and Samuel went back to the living area and huddled together. Samuel took Esther's hand and began to lead them in prayer. "Dear Lord, I know that you can hear and see us. I praise you for your grace and love. We ask now that you come into our hearts and our home and comfort our mom. She really needs you. She hurts so much and just wants to see our dad again. Please just take good care of her. In Jesus name we pray, Amen."

One Saturday morning, Esther was helping her mom do household chores when she found four letters tucked in the bible on the bookshelf. The bible was old and falling apart and they had been so busy trying to transition from having her father around to him being absent that they really didn't have time to sit down and do bible study like they normally did as a family. Usually by the time her mother got home, she grabbed the cold dinner that Esther had put to the side for her and went to bed.

The four letters that Esther found were each folded neatly with her name, Samuel, Ruth, and my beloved written on them. All Esther could do was drop to her knees as she realized that the letters were written in her father's handwriting. Naomi came in at that very moment and when she saw Esther on the floor, she immediately asked her what was wrong. Esther couldn't manage to make a single sound; all she could do was show her mother the letters.

Naomi collapsed immediately onto the floor next to Esther and began to cry. She thought she had finally managed to get control of her emotions when thinking and talking about her husband after a month. But once she saw the handwriting she began to bawl like a baby all over again. Taking the letter addressed to "my beloved" and with shaking hands she composed herself enough to open it. Inside she found these words:

> The love of my life, my wife, my soul mate, my best friend, the mother of my children; you are all of these things and so much more to me. I couldn't find the words to express how I feel out loud so I decided to write these final letters to you and the kids that I knew you wouldn't find until after I was already gone. I prayed, begged, and pleaded with God to deliver and

heal me for this illness and He did just that. Then he told me that it would be short lived. Of course this was an answer that I didn't like, but I knew and still know that He knows what's best. He answered my prayer and told me that He knows the plans that He has for me. While I would be leaving from this Earth, He would be here with you and the children. I know that there was a reason why we were separated after only a short time. I know that God had/has a master plan for all of our lives but it doesn't keep me from grieving when I think of having to leave you alone. You have given me more in these 19 years than anyone else could have given me in hundreds of years. I am so glad that God chose you to be my wife and I am the most blessed man to have been able to share the joys and sorrows of life with you. Each day hasn't been the best but we have managed to stay in love with God and each other through all the heartache. Although I am gone in the physical, please take comfort in knowing that I am free from all suffering now. If you look on the bookshelf where you found these letters you will see a box marked beef jerky and inside you will find some money that I have been setting aside for a while. I wanted to be able to buy you another ring and take you somewhere for our anniversary but as I already said, God had other plans. Please remember me always as I will take your love with me. Kiss the kids for me every night and let them know that there is no one that meant more to me than they have. I have faith and know that God will be with you all where I cannot be because He loves you more than I ever could. I am yours forever.

Until we meet again my love,

Isaiah

# Chapter Ten

# *Lessons Learned*

After reading the letter Isaiah wrote for her, Naomi went to her room and laid on the bed. She held the letter in her hand and silently sobbed as she prayed that God would heal the wound that the loss of her other half left. She felt God wrapping His arms around her which only made her sob from the depths of her soul. As she lay there, she relived every moment of her life with Isaiah. She remembered his scent and the way she felt when he would touch her. She smiled when she thought of how terrified he looked when she was in labor with Samuel and how he looked like a professional by the time Esther came along.

She was so lost in her own grief and thoughts that she didn't bother to talk to Esther about her letter. But she looked forward to the time when the loss of her love Isaiah wouldn't take her breath away and make her want to die with him. In the beginning, she visited his grave site everyday and planted flowers. Lately she has found herself too exhausted to venture there as often. But she always carries Isaiah in her heart and she would never forget him.

One thing Naomi was grateful for was that Isaiah had been with her through some of the teenage years with the kids. Esther, however, didn't feel she had enough time with her father during this time and missed him that much more. She was going through the phase when she liked boys but understood nothing about them. The more she tried to understand about them and to get information from Samuel, the less she got and the more confused she became. She just finally decided that maybe it wasn't time for her to be dealing with boys.

She really missed and prayed that her father could somehow be with her. She felt lonely and missed the days when she could sit in his lap and listen to him tell bible stories. It seemed that at that time all was right with the world but the moment that he died, the world she knew did too. Because her mother spent so much time working, Esther tried to help out around the house. She knew how to cook and clean and so she tried to keep her mother from having to do those duties as much as she could.

Samuel was handy because their dad taught him how to do some things around the house so he took care of anything that broke around the house. Esther took the time to teach Ruth how to wash, hang, and fold laundry. So everybody pitched in and did their part to try and make the load easier to bear. At the end of the day all you would hear was snoring because everybody in the house had worked so hard during the day that as soon as their heads hit the pillow they were out.

Each day got easier and the sting of missing her father became easier to deal with. Esther knew that she would never get over it completely but she trusted that God had a plan for taking her father at such an early age. She just wished she knew exactly what that reason was because it would help ease her grief; or so she thought. Esther met a couple of girls and had really taken a liking to Abigail, the neighbor, but with her father passing there left little time to hang out and talk to her friends.

Esther felt totally alone but she knew that God was there despite how she felt because she could feel His arms around her. She knew that God had her best interest at heart and when the time was right, it would be revealed to her and her family exactly what God's plan is. In the mean time, Esther couldn't help but to feel grateful that her father had instilled God into her and had taught her about the love of God. Because in those lone moments when there was no one around to listen or to care, she knew she could always turn to Him and that everything would be alright.

# Chapter Eleven

# *A New Beginning*

As time and life went on, things became easier for Esther, Samuel, Naomi, and Ruth. Samuel was becoming a man and graduating from High School. He truly missed his father and couldn't help being upset that his father didn't see him make this milestone in his life. At 18 years old, it had been 1 year since his father had died. He couldn't believe so much time had passed but with each day it truly became easier to deal with the loss. He chose to hide in his studies and in household chores.

Samuel tried to help his mother as much as he could with everything even though he knew that she much preferred his father to be there. He truly admired his mother and how strong she was. Samuel studied the bible more intently than ever because he was lacking a father and he needed to know how to be a man and what things men were suppose to do. His father had charged him in his letter with being the head of the household and being a good example to his sisters since he was gone. Samuel tried to step up to the plate and even though at times he felt lost and overwhelmed, overall he thought he had done a good job and that his father would truly be proud of him.

Samuel took a job working at the local market after he was done with school. He wanted to help his mother so that she could let some of the jobs go that she had been working so hard for the past year since his father's death. Naomi had made Samuel promise to focus on finishing school and had instilled that that was more important than making a buck. But it seemed that the day that he finished school, he was lined up in the market ringing up customers. Naomi had insisted that Isaiah would've wanted Samuel to finish school before doing anything else in life; so she made sure that happened.

Although Naomi couldn't resist taking some of Samuel's earnings, at his extreme insistence, she found a way to make him keep the majority of it saved for a rainy day or whatever he wanted to spend it on other than her and household items. Samuel had no idea that his mother was stashing the money he was giving her and not using or spending it until he met and fell in love with Dana.

Samuel met Dana while in school but he was too busy trying to finish that he really hadn't paid her that much attention. One day while working at the market, Dana walked in with her long flowing hair and Samuel's breath caught in his chest. From that moment on they were inseparable. Samuel came up to Naomi one day while Naomi was relaxing on her bed and told her about Dana. Samuel told his mother that he loved Dana and wanted to be her husband.

Naomi was so thrilled and yet a little saddened because her son was truly a man now. So she told him to grab a small beef jerky box that was on the bookshelf and bring it to her. Samuel did as he was told and when he brought the box to his mother, he gasped at what he saw when she opened it. There was thousands of dollars in it. Naomi grabbed $2,000 and told him "Samuel, go into town, buy a nice suit, and go to the jeweler to get a ring because every girl needs to have a ring when you ask for her hand in marriage. I am so proud of the man you have become and I know that your father would be thrilled too." So Samuel did as he was told and came back from town to show his mom the ring he had chosen to give Dana. It was one of the rare moments in the past 2 years that could be considered a good memory. Samuel, 19, was getting married.

Samuel called Dana and asked if she felt like taking a drive. Of course she said yes because she was just as in love with Samuel as he was with her. She had no idea what was awaiting her and when Samuel came to pick her up she blushed and giggled because she had never seen him in a suit. Dana felt a little underdressed and begged Samuel to let her go back inside and change into something dressier. Samuel agreed but said, "Please hurry because we have plans."

Dana went inside and was back out in a jiffy looking more stunning than Samuel could've ever imagined and taking his breath away. Samuel took Dana away in the truck and they went to the park where he pulled a basket from the back of the truck that he had prepared. Dana did not suspect anything and she did not know that Samuel had talked to her father and got the okay to ask for her hand in marriage. Dana was just happy to be in Samuel's company because she truly loved him.

As Samuel and Dana sat on the blanket, stuffed from eating, Samuel got up the nerve to tell her what he really wanted to say. "Pretty brown eyes, my dad taught me before he died that it was important for a man to take pride in his job, his appearance, and his family. Up until now, my family has been my mom and sisters. But now I want to expand my family to include you." Samuel moved to one knee and said "Dana will you make me the happiest man on this side of heaven by being my wife?" Dana was caught off guard and couldn't manage to say anything. All she could do was cry because she knew what all he had gone through with losing his father because they had spent many nights talking about how important he was to Samuel. Dana wiped her eyes, looked at Samuel somberly, and whispered these words "I do."

As if overnight, it was time for Samuel to begin his new life. Isaiah and Naomi had save so much money that they were able to pay to have Samuel and Dana's home built for them. The wedding had been beautiful and now it was time to welcome little Malachi into the world. Naomi thought of Isaiah often because she knew he wouldn't get to meet any of their grandchildren. It had been 3 years now and so much had happened and changed that it seemed more like 90 years. Naomi was enjoying every moment of her life except for those rare moments when her grief for Isaiah crept up on her but those moments had become few and far between. Somehow Naomi had learned to do the impossible; she had learned to live without Isaiah. Each day it became easier and Malachi had become her world. She spent all of her extra time being a grandmother and showering her grandson with all of the love that Isaiah would have. Her days were once again filled with purpose because of this bundle of joy and strangely baby Malachi reminded her of Isaiah.

# Chapter Twelve

## *Abandonment*

Samuel getting married and starting a family was suppose to be a happy occasion for them all because they knew Isaiah would've have been happy. But it was just a reminder for Esther that she was losing another man from her life. Esther always allowed herself to attach to the men in her life because she missed the love that she had for her father. Along with Esther's attachment each time came the possibility for hurt. And each time she attached to a man, it seemed that hurt was all she would get in return. Samuel could no longer help her in the boy department with advice, now she was on her own because he had a wife and family. Her father couldn't give her advice because he left her too. "Why do all the men I love and respect leave me? Is there something wrong with me that keeps them from wanting to be close to me?" were all questions Esther would ask herself in the middle of the night.

Since Esther longed for the relationship and love only a father figure could give her, it was no surprise to her friend Abigail that Esther and Adam seemed to clique immediately. Esther would hang out at Abigail's house so that they could work on homework together but they would always find Adam peeking around corners at them working. "You know my brother thinks you are cute, right?" Abigail asked Esther one day while they were over studying. Esther hadn't paid much attention to Adam because in her mind he was just another man for her to love and for him to walk away. Even though Abigail and Esther spent so much time together, they hadn't really talked about Esther's feelings concerning men. This was mainly because coming to Abigail's house was an escape from her everyday reality, feelings of rejection, and loneliness. Now that Abigail brought this to Esther's attention, it seemed that each time she would look around Adam was coming around offering something to drink or just trying to be apart of their conversation. Esther and Abigail would giggle together at first because Adam would be trying to be so smooth that he really didn't realize how silly he sounded. But after a while, Esther began to entertain the thought of being Adam's friend. She really could use someone to talk to about her feelings.

So one day while leaving Abigail's house, Esther decided to give Adam's friendship a try. Esther found Adam in the backyard laying on the grass and looking up at the stars. Esther walked over and asked "Do you mind if I sit down for a bit?" Adam's reply was to smile and move over on the blanket to make room for her to sit down. Esther laid down on the blanket too and began dazing at the stars. Esther began to think about heaven and wonder if her father could see her down here. She began to wonder if he had any idea just how much she truly missed him. All the times they just played together, when she would hurt herself and her dad would pick her up; she truly was his princess. Esther missed the moments when her father would just spend time with her and they would talk about how he knew God was real.

All of these things went through her head and then she decided to speak. "Adam, do you think God is real?" she asked. Adam sat up and contemplated the question. He really wondered what would make someone ask him a question like that. "Yes, I believe that God exists. I don't always understand how He is in more than one place at a time, looking at everyone, feeling everything they feel. But, yes, I do believe. Why do you ask?" Adam replied. "All of my life I have been taught that God exists, that He looks down on us, feels what we feel, and that He has a master plan for each of our lives.

The only thing is sometimes I wonder if He truly is real; why didn't He heal my father? Why didn't He keep my father alive so that my mother and I wouldn't have to live without him? If He feels everything I feel, why didn't He feel my heart break apart on the night that I watched my father die? Why didn't He see that we would be lost and in pain when he was gone? Why did He take my brother away from me? He was the next best thing I had to a father and my father's blood runs through his veins.

How could He leave me all alone with my pain if He loves me? What kind of plan could He possibly have for me?" she asked.

Halfway through her questions, Esther hadn't noticed that tears were flowing down her face but Adam had noticed. And because somehow along the way he began to truly care for her, he began to pull her close to comfort her. He could feel the deep hurt that she had tried to hide from everybody for so long. He could tell that if she ever had the chance to meet God face to face, she would've asked Him all these questions and probably more. He knew that he couldn't take her pain away but at that moment he decided he wanted to be a protector of her heart. He never again wanted to see her cry and grieve this way. He wanted to be the one that was different than all the rest of the men in her life; he wanted to be the one that stayed.

"Esther, I can't answer some of the questions you have. I can't take your pain away. If you would let me try I would like to love you. I would like to be your friend. When you are ready, I would like you to carry my last name as well. Please, Esther, will you give me a chance to show you what it feels like to have someone that is different for a change?" Adam asked. Esther pondered what her answer should be because she really didn't want to put her feelings out there again to be hurt by another man but then again she hadn't planned to tell anyone the true secrets that her heart contained. Now that she had, there was no going back. Maybe she should trust Adam because she had already trusted him with more than she trusted anybody else with. "Sure Adam, we can try." Esther replied.

# Chapter Thirteen

# *An Unexpected Surprise*

*E*sther and Adam began to date and as they grew closer, Esther's sense of security grew larger. She began to trust men again and even God. No longer was she angry with Him for taking away all of the influential people in her life that she truly cared for. She began to believe in God again because she knew it had to be Him that brought Adam to her. He was so caring and he truly wooed her. Adam would bring flowers every time they would go out on a date. Esther trusted Adam with all that she had which was saying a lot because before that night in the yard, she hadn't trusted anyone. Somehow Adam managed to do every thing he promised to do and he did show her that he was different.

Esther fell in love with Adam and Adam was in love with her. Adam listened to her, shared his hopes and dreams with her, helped calm her fears, and helped her live a life filled with adventure. Esther actually was happy to be alive again; she felt like she was doing more than just merely existing. She was living and loving and having fun doing all of it. Ever so often, Esther would think of her father and on those nights Adam had to pull out all the stops to cheer her up. The main thing Adam tried to remind Esther was that her father wouldn't have wanted her sad over here all of these years later. But regardless, Adam was there to talk whenever she needed someone and she spent a lot of time telling her mother Naomi about him.

So it was no surprise to her mother when Adam asked for Esther's hand in marriage. Naomi knew how much Adam meant to Esther and so she gave her blessing to him. Not long after their marriage, Esther became pregnant with two beautiful twins; a daughter named Mary and a son named Peter. Life with Adam was wonderful and everyday was filled with adventure. It was everything that he had promised and so much more. Esther never knew that love like this existed. The love she had for Adam and her children encompassed her entire heart and there was little room for anybody else.

Esther was content for the first time because she was able to love her babies and she took pride in being able to talk to them about her father. Adam would work so that Esther could stay at home until the kids became school aged. When they were old enough for school,

Esther decided to find a job so she would have something to do during the days. Life was wonderful and she once again believed all of the things she had been told since she was a child about God's grace, mercy, and love. She believed it because she saw it at work in her life everyday.

## Chapter Fourteen

## *Unraveling Changes*

Until one day Esther woke up to find that the perfect life she thought she and Adam shared didn't really exist. Adam was gone. He didn't leave a note to say where he had gone and after 2 weeks had gone by and he still hadn't returned she decided it was time to move on. Mary and Peter would ask where Adam was all of the time in the beginning but after a month of asking non-stop for their father, Esther decided to tell them that he had died. She knew this was a lie but it was so much easier than telling the truth. The truth was that Adam lied and he left her just like all the rest.

Adam quite possibly was worse than the rest of the men because he promised to stay. Maybe he got overwhelmed and decided the relationship was too much for him. But how could he just walk away from the kids this way. He didn't even say goodbye. How was she supposed to explain the fact that their father didn't want the perfect life they had anymore? Esther was deeply hurt all over again. She had trusted him with all of him. She trusted him to be different; but she realized he is just like everybody else. How could he lie to her and make her believe in God again when he had no intention of staying?

Esther put herself through these questions everyday for weeks. At night after she would put the kids to bed, she and a glass of wine or tequila would curl up by the fire. The alcohol seemed to seal the hurt that she felt. She never let the kids see her this way but it was okay to get her through the night. She just needed to make it through the night without thinking about her broken heart. Esther would fall asleep fairly easy but it was the waking up alone with the kids that would drive her back to the same place again night after night.

Trying to raise them with no help; too afraid to trust anybody ever again and definitely not God because He had let her down too many times already. The only difference between her father leaving and Adam leaving was that her father didn't have a choice but to leave. Adam had a choice and he chose to walk away. Until that day, Esther thought they were both happy with the life they had built together. All Esther could think was that if it wasn't for her job at the local dentist as a receptionist, she wouldn't be able to provide for her kids. Adam left them with nothing and she didn't expect to ever hear from him again.

Esther went to her mother Naomi and began to explain what happened with Adam. Naomi was furious but instead of saying "I told you so" she just said "how can I help make things easier on you and my babies, Esther?" For this and so much more, Esther knew she would love her mother forever. At every stage in her life where she was tremendously hurt, her mother had come to her rescue. Now with the loss of another love from her life, here was her mother again to save the day.

Grateful and overwhelmed Esther began to sob into her mother's shoulder while all the grief and pain overtook her all at once. Naomi stroked her precious daughter's shoulder and told her "everything would be just fine. God's got it all in His hands and He won't put more on you than you can bear to stand." It wasn't until that very moment that Esther began to see things truly from her mother's perspective and began to wonder how in the world her mother could stay so optimistic despite the world around her falling completely apart. She admired her mother's strength and courage and took pride in knowing that she was built from that same stock. Esther pulled herself together, wiped the tears from her eyes, and decided at that very moment that she would never again shed a tear over love lost. She decided that all she needed was her two kids, her God, and her family. Never again would she allow a man to make her grieve in this way.

# Chapter Fifteen

## *Picking Up The Pieces*

Waking up from the dream world that she had been in for the past 7 years was the rudest awakening that she had ever experienced. But it was so important for her children that she finally awaken from it and begin to live life based on reality. And the reality of it was that it was up to her to provide and safe and happy home for her children and herself. Esther pulled herself together and decided to deal with the reality of her feelings instead of trying to drown them in a sea of alcohol.

Esther began to pray nightly again for the pain to leave because that's all she knew to do. If her mother could get through losing her father, she definitely could get over losing Adam. So as time went on Esther began to pray for God to make her a better mother and to rebuild her trust in Him instead of men. Overall, Esther had no regrets in life except for one; she wished that she could've still carried on the tradition that her father instilled in them from the beginning and taught her children about God. At this point in her life, it was like starting over but she had to do it in order to regain some sense of normalcy for herself. So Esther began to pull Mary and Peter around so that they could begin learning about the ways and love of God.

Everything was going well and after a while they actually were able to build bible study into their daily routine. Mary and Peter were really excited to study the bible because it was something different that they had never experienced before. By studying with the kids, Esther saw that God uses whomever He can to get whatever He needs done. She began to understand that the grief she felt when her father initially passed from this life would not have happened if she understood that God had a place reserved for his children in Heaven. One thing Esther knew if she didn't know anything else was that her father went to Heaven because God truly loved him.

One day while going through old boxes to pack up all of Adam's things, Esther came across the letter that her father wrote her. Esther didn't know what it contained because she never opened it out of fear. Esther decided that now was the time to take that leap and see what her father wrote to her.

Esther,

My dear sweet baby girl; you have brought me more happiness than I ever thought possible. I don't know how I ever got along without you being in my life. You stormed into me and your mother's life out of the blue and I am so glad that you did. My prayer for you has always been that God will bless you in abundance, that He protects you, and wrap you in His loving arms as He has done for me. I am so sorry my little girl that I can't be there for you when you have your first boyfriend, your first kiss, your first dance, your first heartbreak, your first love, and your first baby. What saddens me even more than this is that I can't be there with you when you walk down the aisle to your prince charming. I can promise you one think, I promise to look down on you from Heaven. I promise that you will feel my love at every stage in your life. I promise that Our Heavenly Father will take care of you and love you. Don't ever settle for less that Our Heavenly Father's love. The perfect man that He has for you will love you unconditionally, nurture you, protect you, provide for you, respect you, love you, and never desert you. He will treat you the same way that I treated you and your mother while I was here. That is why I did it so that you could have the perfect example of a true man of God. I want you to have a man after God's own heart; after my own heart. I am so sorry that I can't give you all the advice that you should receive from me. Just know I love you now and forever.

Love always,
Daddy

Esther began to break down halfway through the letter because she realized that her father knew every moment of her life before she even got there. She missed her father more than words could express and longed for the days when she could sit on his lap and cry about whatever hadn't gone the way she hoped it would. She remembered even as an early teenager sitting on her father's lap telling him about her day. She truly knew that she was loved by her father and had no doubt that every word he spoke in his letter was his heart's desire. It broke her heart all over again but yet she could smile at all the memories he left her with.

At the end of the day, death had her father but life lived on in her memories of him. It seemed like forever ago that her father had passed from this life into the next and yet it sometimes seemed like everyday was the day after he died. The days to live in oblivion had long since passed and now all that remained was reality. Even as time passed and the kids grew older, it became harder for Esther to manage on her own. She knew that she didn't have what she needed to teach her son how to be a man; the only thing she could do was teach him how to treat a woman. Yet each time she thought of giving her heart away to another, she cringed. Esther decided to pray to God for strength and relief. That would give her the courage to get through until the next hurdle came. Esther knew like it or not; the next hurdle would come.

## Chapter Sixteen

## *The Storm*

*E*sther instilled in her kids the importance of loving God and praying to Him daily so that He could be a part of every phase in their lives. Esther taught them how to look out for one another because family was all you had at the end of the day. Overall Mary and Peter were good kids and they were usually obedient to whatever Esther instructed them to do. Mary and Peter loved to swim in the lake a mile from home with their friends from school but Esther was afraid something would happen and so instructed them to wait on her to take them each time.

One day all the kid in the neighborhood were going to the lake and Mary and Peter didn't want to feel left out because their mom was at work so they decided to go swimming in the lake too. On this particular day the sun was really hot and so the cool water felt wonderful against their skin as they swung from the rope and landed in the lake. Some years earlier older kids tied the rope securely to a tree so that it would be like diving. Mary, Peter, and the other kids from the neighborhood took turns swinging in and doing flips. Everything was going wonderfully until Mary struck her head against a rock on the last swing in and plopped into the water.

Peter too busy having fun didn't notice it until he looked around for her and couldn't find her. Mary had fallen into the lake and sank to the bottom. Peter began to panic because he didn't know how long she had been down there or how to help her. Immediately the atmosphere changed from a joyous one filled with laughter to a solemn one where someone may be dead. Peter dived in the lake and swam to his twin sister. They had always been joined at the hip since being in their mother's womb. All kinds of things ran through his head as he raced to save his sister.

Peter got to her and carried her back to the surface where he laid her on the ground on her side. One of the other kids had run to get their father while Peter went to get Mary and it was a good thing because he was able to administer CPR on her. The water was expelled from Mary's body but she still hadn't woken up. The neighborhood kid's father grabbed Mary and put her in his truck to rush her into town to the hospital. While all of this was going on Peter ran

*The Storm*

all the way into town to get his mother and let her know what had happened. He knew she would be furious because of her previous instructions to them but he couldn't keep this from her.

As soon as Peter arrived in the dentist lobby, Esther knew something wasn't right. He was out of breath and more importantly she didn't see Mary. "Where's your sister, Peter and what's wrong?" she asked. Peter didn't realize it but somewhere along the way he had began to cry while he ran the 4 miles into town to his mother's job. Tears streaming down his face and his heart overwhelmed with hurt, he began to explain to his mother what happened at the lake and where Mr. George had taken Mary. Without an ounce of hesitation, Esther grabbed her bag, told her boss she had to go, took Peter and ran to her car to go to her baby.

All the way to the hospital, Esther could only think about all of the pain and suffering she had already experienced and that her heart couldn't bare anything else. Esther and Peter ran into the hospital and gave the nurse at the front desk Mary's name. The nurse told them that she was in surgery and that she would take them to the holding area for emergency patients. As Esther and Peter sat in the waiting area, all kinds of painful thoughts crossed their minds. Esther wanted to fuss at Peter because she had specifically told them not to go without her but she saw no real purpose in doing that now because what was most important was her baby being okay. So wait was what they did with neither of them uttering a single word. They both silently prayed that the grace of God would extend to Mary even while she was going through surgery.

## Chapter Seventeen

## *Not Again*

The only thing the nurse had told them was that Mary was in pretty rough shape when she was brought in and they didn't know what that meant. They were so busy in their own thoughts that they didn't see Mr. George sitting in the emergency room kneeling in the corner praying for Mary as well. Mr. George was an older gentleman who loved all the neighborhood kids and did what he could to help and encourage them. He looked up and saw Esther and Peter sitting there in a daze and decided to leave them alone for now.

At the same time, the doctor came out of the double doors and began walking towards the waiting area. As soon as the doctor came through the doors, Esther noticed the defeated look on his face and thought please don't be looking for me. As if the doctor could read her thoughts he looked straight into her eyes and she new immediately that Mary was gone. Instantly Esther broke apart at the despair that gripped her heart took over her entire being. Esther began to sob uncontrollably and as the doctor started talking because he had to say the words, Esther began to clutch her chest in pain. Her heart was literally breaking because Mary and Peter were all that she had left to live for and now one of the things that made her heart keep beating was gone.

It was like a dream and the doctor was speaking in slow motion when he let Esther know that Mary had suffered a major hemorrhage when she struck her head on the rock. The hemorrhage was unrepairable and the amount of water that she took into her already weakened state was too much for her teenage body to handle. Mary died on the operating room table. Esther began to cry aloud at this point because it was her only release from the pain that she felt inside.

If she tried to hold it in anymore, she felt that her body would split into two pieces. Peter sat next to where she and the doctor stood crying because he felt like it was his fault. It was his responsibility to protect his sister. He was the man of the house; he had failed in his main duty. He couldn't take back what had happened and now his mother couldn't stop her heart from breaking. How could Mary be so alive and well one moment and in a split second it be over? No one understood and Esther was so grief stricken that she didn't feel Mr. George wrap his arms around her.

The pain consumed every part of her and would not let go. The doctor yelled for a nurse to bring a sedative because Esther would be spending the night under the hospital's supervision; the doctor feared what the pain of losing a child would do to her. The nurse came immediately with a gurney and sedated Esther to help her cope with the pain and grief she felt. Before Esther fell asleep she remembered thinking this is a pain no one should ever feel.

## Chapter Eighteen

## *Reality Sets In*

*E*sther awoke the next day in a hospital and the idea that this was all a dream slowly became a reality for her. Esther had tried everything she could not to let the pressure and pain of this life get to her. She maintained her faith and trust in God even though she didn't have a clue about the plan that He had for her. But this broke that silence and she began to pray aloud, "Not again, Jesus. Why, God? Why!!!! She was just a child; she was just my child. We have endured enough heartache. Please just tell me why. What is your plan for my life and why does there have to be so much pain in the midst of it? What did I do to deserve the level of heartache I have suffered? I didn't say much when you took my daddy. I just said it was God's will and in His plan. I didn't say anything when Adam left. Mama told me that you have a plan and maybe Adam wasn't a part of that plan. But now one of the most precious gifts you gave me is gone and will never return. How can I believe you love me truly and deeply when you keep taking everything from me? Everyone I love leaves and it's not fair. How am I to love someone when that someone keeps going away? Please just talk to me."

"Explain your purpose to me. Let me see your plan for my life. Help me understand. Please, God, I have never asked for anything but this one thing I need. I have to understand what is happening and why. I am so sorry for everything I did. I tried to do right. I tried to make you proud. You promised to take care of me and I trusted you for that too even when I didn't understand. I need you; please don't forsake me now because I can't understand. I don't want to accept reality. It's more than I can take."

Clear as a bell, Esther heard God speak to her. "Alright, my child, I have held my tongue long enough. I do have a plan for your life. If I told you what it was when I called your father and daughter home or when I removed Adam from you life, you wouldn't have understood. I promise you that I do love you and I know the plans that I have for you. It is plans for a hope and a future. Just trust me; I promise never to leave or forsake you. It will all work out in the end for your good. Trust me."

Esther was caught off guard by this immediately reply that she just sat on the hospital bed in disbelief and amazement. Her soul felt that God truly loved her because He replied to her immediately and yet her mind still had a few questions. Esther knew this was a time for true faith to step in and conquer her fears and mistrust. So now it was time to deal in faith instead of reality or fantasy.

## Chapter Nineteen

## *Trying Again*

Several months passed by since Mary's death and some days Esther was okay but on other days it was too much to handle. On those rough nights she would find herself seeking solitude in a glass of wine. This always seemed to help her feel better when Adam first left her. But the next morning, Esther always felt the sting of loss over her again. After months of trying to hide behind a bottle of alcohol, Esther decided that she could no longer do that. She had to deal with the loss now no matter how much it hurt her. Hiding away was no longer working and it wasn't good for Peter to see her going down this path.

"I am a grown woman, a mother, and a child of God. I have to pull it together because neither my father nor Mary would've wanted this for me. God you alone know the amount of pain I am experiencing and that I have agonized over for half of my life. I just want things to be okay again. Just make things okay again. I miss her smile. I miss the way my father's stomach sounded when it rumbled. I miss him sneaking in my bedroom at night and stroking my head while whispering I love you to the moon and back. I find it so hard to function, God. I don't want to be bitter and damaged; I want to feel whole again. Please take this pain away" she said during a moment of clarity.

Esther did all that she could do to keep Peter from slumping into a state of depression but it was exhausting trying to encourage him when she didn't feel encouraged some days. Esther reminded herself of the words that God had spoken to her months prior and she wanted Peter to have the same encounter with God. Peter had finally gone back to school but he lacked his normal spunk and she truly wished that she knew the right words to say to Peter to make him feel better. She found herself constantly reminding him that it wasn't his fault but she didn't feel as if he believed her. She knew he was suffering severely because Mary and Peter had been together since being in her womb. There was no way to get over that bond overnight.

Esther found herself praying more and more for Peter's safety, sanity, and encouragement than even her own. After having this experience with God, she knew there was no way He wouldn't feel and hear Peter's prayers and pain. After all, He had heard hers and come to see about her immediately.

It took some time and a lot of prayer, but Peter and Esther finally began to settle into a routine that didn't involve Mary. Although they thought of her frequently, there wasn't as much pain as there previously had been. Peter was getting ready to graduate high school but all this did was refresh the pain for them both. Esther often wondered what Mary would have looked like in her cap and gown, on her wedding day, as she bore her children. Esther was determined not to let this consume her because she knew where those thoughts led to; back to the pain that she felt she had escaped from.

Instead, Esther chose to focus on the achievement that Peter had made. It amazed her that he was still able to finish school as one of the top people in his class despite the tragedy that had pained him a couple of years earlier. But he had done it and now it was time for him to start his life in college. Peter was starting his new life and Esther was going to be on her own for the first time in her life. She didn't have a husband because a few months after leaving them, her mother said that there was a story in the paper where he had been killed in a motorcycle accident. She didn't have a child to tend to anymore because Peter was going away to college and Mary was no longer alive. So Esther decided to take time to grow her relationship with God. Ever so often she would miss the companionship that a husband gave but she had suffered more in the love department than she wanted to or even thought possible.

# Chapter 20

# *The Meaning of it All*

As the time passed by, Esther tried to spend her weekends at the beach. It gave her time to think about life and it reminded her of when she was younger and her father was still alive. She, Samuel, and Ruth would run up and down the beach chasing seagulls and collecting seashells. During those days she didn't have a care in the world. She enjoyed spending the time with her family and the serenity of the ocean water coming to the shore and returning to the ocean calmed her soul. Esther watched the sun set and rise on most weekends and then after two months of travelling to the beach each weekend, she made a major decision.

Esther decided to move to a house on the beach. This way she could leave behind all the bad memories and the constant reminders that pain was all this life had to offer. When the tide was high,

Esther would stand on the porch of the beach house so that she could marvel at God. It was during these moments that she knew God truly existed and was capable of doing beautiful things even though her life hadn't seen many of those beautiful things. Esther began to wonder why she hadn't been able to experience this beauty in her life. Feeling hurt, Esther went to bed and decided she wouldn't think about those things.

The next day Esther couldn't shake her feelings from the night before. So she took to the beach yet again hoping the waves would calm her hurting heart. As she sat on the beach, she began to think about her life and how she got to this point. The full moon is bright and shining and the tide is high. The waves are splashing against the rocks and the beams of the pier. She contemplates jumping in to finally be free from the strife that has consumed her for all of her life. She has been sitting here for what seems like days but in fact it's only been 3 hours. She has watched the families picnicking and the children screeching with joy at all the sights and wonders this world holds. It amazed Esther that someone could be so naïve and oblivious to everything that was going on around them.

Esther watches the family as they leave and the sun sets with vibrant colors of purple, pink, and orange. She knows that God is real every time she thinks of the splendor and wonder that He is.

But she couldn't stop the feelings from coming back. She began wondering if God is real, then why had she suffered so much pain and anguish in her lifetime. Nightfall comes and she sees her reflection in the water. She marvels at how the years and pain have added wrinkles to her face and hands. Her hair once black and flowing is now gray and leaving. Her womb once alive and in full season is now closed and she is barren. Finally the contemplation becomes more than a thought and is now her jumping off the pier into the raging ocean. Instead of swimming, Esther just drifted to the bottom of the ocean floor.

# Chapter 21

## *Clarity for the Pain*

Solomon decided to go for a midnight stroll along the beach. He sat on the deck of his ocean front condo for hours trying to figure out what his next move would be and where he would go next. He had traveled the world looking for the feeling of ecstasy that he hoped he would find in a job working at the mill, farming the land and grooming horses, or finding love in Magdalene. Somehow he ended up at this condo in Florida and he wasn't quite sure how he still felt empty after having lived a full life according to many men's standards. As Solomon is walking he notices some foot prints in the sand.

Out of curiosity, he follows the foot prints on the beach to a woman that is sitting above him on the pier. Solomon can only think one thing that this woman is breathtaking. Just as he thinks this,

Solomon sees Esther jump in. Wondering if she is crazy to jump into the ocean when the tide is high, his mind tells him to turn and walk away. Only his body won't allow him to move a muscle and then he realizes why. "This woman hasn't come back to the surface, dear God, I have to help her" Solomon says aloud. So without reluctance Solomon dives off the beach sands into the water in search of this woman.

He is so happy that the moon is high because this gives him the light that he needs to try and find her. Solomon doesn't realize it but he swims directly to the bottom of the ocean floor and finds Esther there. He pulls her up to the surface and they make there way back to the shore. "What were you thinking woman? Are you crazy?" he yelled at her though panting breaths. Esther just looked at him wondering where he came from. If it hadn't been for this man seeing her and coming to save her, she would've met her maker and been able to ask him all of the questions she had been wanting to since she was a kid.

"No, I am not crazy man. One would think that you are because you jumped in behind me. Who are you?" Esther asked. Solomon replied, "My name is Solomon. I was walking along the beach and I saw you jump in. When I didn't see you resurface I tried to help you." "My name is Esther and thanks for jumping in but I didn't need your help. I was just fine on my own", Esther replied. Solomon stood up and said "Next time I won't help you then. Good night Ms. Esther." With that Solomon left her sitting on the beach soaking wet to think.

Thinking is exactly what Esther did too. Thinking aloud she began asking "Who does this man think he is? He seemed kind of snooty. But then again he was handsome and I did like the way he picked me when he thought he was rescuing me. Oh who am I kidding? He could never see anything in me. I am an old, washed up, scarred woman. Who could want someone like me?" The only problem was that Solomon and Esther were the only two people on the beach and Solomon was still within ear shot of Esther.

Solomon had heard everything she said and he couldn't help but to smile because he was wondering who wouldn't find her attractive. She was beautiful outside and now that he had heard what she said he understood why she had been so short with him. He could see her inside and knew it was just as beautiful as her outside; she just had been wounded pretty badly. Just as he was thinking that God whispered to him, "That's the one for you. She is your Eve." Solomon smiled because he had been asking God to bring someone into his life that he could share his love with.

He promised God after Magdalene that he wouldn't look anymore because he had gotten hurt by that relationship. He knew all too familiarly what hurt and pain looked like. He knew what it felt like to give his all and have the other person not care at all. So he prayed and told God that he was done unless he showed him someone different. "Really? Her? She's already been hurt too badly. Anyway, I will follow your words." God looked down on His son and smiled as his submissiveness to His will. Knowing the perfect plan that He formed since before the world began for both Esther and Solomon gave Him great pleasure.

## Chapter 22

## *Amazing is His Grace*

*E*sther began to walk the beach at night more than usual in hopes that she would run into the handsome stranger. About a week had gone by since she had seen him and she was beginning to wonder if she would see him again. Then one night while looking up at the stars a familiar voice spoke to her, "Hey stranger. Where have you been?" Solomon asked. Esther turned around suddenly as she was shocked to hear his voice and yet thrilled at the same time which is why she had a gigantic smile across her face.

Esther thought about the smooth way Solomon's voice glazed across her eardrum and she couldn't help but to grin. "Hey, Solomon, I have just been enjoying life the best way I know how. How have you been?" Esther inquired. "I haven't been able to take my mind off of you, would you like to go for a walk?" Solomon asked. Esther only shook her head yes as Solomon held out his hand to help her get up from the rock she had been sitting on. Esther had no idea that this would be the beginning of many more walks to come but Solomon knew because God had already whispered those words to him.

As they walked, Solomon did most of the talking about his life so far and the events that led him to this place of solitude. He talked of his hopes and dreams, his desire to have children but never being able to find the right one to have them with, and the failures of his life. Solomon had suffered heartache just like Esther had and knew all too well what it felt like not to be wanted. All Esther could think was that Solomon was an open book and he didn't mind telling her the intimate details of his life. They enjoyed each others company so much so that every evening at sun set they would meet at the same rock to walk and talk together.

What started off as a wonderful friendship quickly began to become more for them both. Only Esther was terrified because of the promise she made to herself years earlier and yet she couldn't help smiling each time she thought about Solomon. There was a sense of serenity that remained in his voice no matter how painful she thought the experience he described would have been for him. It amazed Esther that Solomon could be so calm about the pain he had endured in his life. All the things he talked about from his childhood up until this very moment mirrored Esther's life so much it was scary. But one thing that remained constant in Solomon's life was that he trusted God will all of his being despite the challenges that life brought about.

Esther wanted to run as far away as she could from the feelings of love that were beginning to form between Solomon and her but it was like a magnet was pulling the two of them closer together. No matter how much she wanted to pull apart so that she could keep her heart from being broken again, she couldn't. Esther decided to pray and ask God for a sign that she and Solomon were to pursue the feelings they had for each other. The sign came that night while Esther was asleep.

God visited her in a dream and showed her a vision of her wedding day. Esther thought this was really funny especially considering the man she was marrying looked nothing like Adam; he strangely resembled Solomon. In her dream she felt a sense of calm wash over her and she could hear God telling her that He had been preparing her for this moment for her entire life. All of the things that had happened, all of the pain that she had suffered was to bring Solomon and her together as one. It was to show Esther God's amazing grace that He knew was sufficient enough to erase all of the pain, all of her flaws, remove all of her fears, heal her heart that once was falling apart, and show her the love that He has for her. God had spent the years grooming Solomon to be strong enough to help calm Esther's fears and wipe her tears away. God specifically designed Solomon for Esther and Esther for Solomon.

Esther awoke with a start and as her mind tried to comprehend everything that she felt and saw in her dream, her heart and soul knew that all of it was real. Esther had spent so much time wondering what God's plan was for her that she never could've foreseen this would be the reason for it all. The love that she felt for Solomon was one that she had never before felt and she knew that it was real. For the first time in her life, she wanted to step out on faith and allow God's amazing grace to save and restore her.

So Esther got out of bed and walked over to Solomon's beach house. She knocked on the door and as he saw Esther, he already knew what God had done. He began to smile because he saw this beautiful woman that God had created just for him. He knew that she was his and he was hers. There was no need to let time pass them by because he trusted God completely and he immediately asked Esther to be his wife. Esther turned her back on Solomon and pretended to think about it for a moment, just to tease him. Then slowly turning around with tears in her eyes, "yes" was her reply.